THE ART OF SIMPLE LIVING

Declutter Your Life, Embrace Calmness, Reignite Happiness, and Experience Lasting Inner Harmony.

PRADIP DAS

Please see the Author Profile

Table of Contents

Introduction

In the heart of a small village lived a man named Mohandas. He wasn't rich, nor did he have much of what the world considered valuable. But there was something extraordinary about him that touched the lives of everyone around him.

Mohandas believed in the power of simplicity. His clothes were plain, and his belongings were few. People often wondered why he chose to live this way. Mohandas, who later became known as Mahatma Gandhi, was on a profound journey to discover the art of simple living.

The story begins in the city of Porbandar, where Mohandas was born. From a young age, he showed kindness to all, treating everyone with respect, regardless of their background. His heart was filled with empathy, and he felt deeply for the struggles of those around him.

As Mohandas grew older, he went to distant lands to study. He encountered new cultures and different ways of life. However, the more he saw, the more he felt a growing sense of disconnection. It was during these travels that he began to question the complexities of modern living and longed for a life that resonated with authenticity.

One day, while sitting on a quiet riverbank, Mohandas experienced a deep realization. He understood that true happiness didn't come from material possessions or societal expectations. Instead, it came from a life of purpose, love, and connection. This was the beginning of his quest for the art of simple living.

Mohandas returned to India, inspired to lead a life aligned with his newfound beliefs. He wore simple, homespun clothes, developd his own food, and chose a lifestyle that minimized harm to the environment. People began to take notice of this man who lived with such authenticity, and the message of simple living echoed far and wide.

Mohandas, now known as Mahatma Gandhi, became a symbol of hope and resilience. His commitment to nonviolence and simplicity became the guiding light for millions seeking a meaningful way of life.

Gandhi's story teaches us that the art of simple living is not about deprivation but about finding richness in what truly matters. It's about embracing a life of purpose, empathy, and gratitude. As we go deep into the principles of simplicity, let us draw inspiration from Gandhi's journey and discover the joy that comes from living a life of authenticity and simplicity.

In a world that often equates success and happiness with material possessions, it can be difficult to imagine that living with less could actually lead to greater fulfillment. Yet, the simple living thoughts have been gaining momentum in recent years, with more and more people embracing the idea that less truly can be more.

At its core, simplify your life and focusing on what truly matters. It's about decluttering your physical space, but also decluttering your mind and your schedule. It's about being intentional with your time, your money, and your energy, and directing those resources toward the things that bring you the most joy and fulfillment.

So why does simple living matter? There are countless reasons, but some of the most compelling include:

Simple living helps you focus on your priorities. By cutting out the excess and the distractions, you can hone in on the things that truly matter to you, whether that's spending time with loved ones, pursuing a passion project, or simply enjoying moments of peace and quiet.

Simple living reduces stress and anxiety. When we're surrounded by clutter and constantly bombarded with information, it can be hard to find a sense of calm. Simplifying your life can help you feel more centered and grounded, and give you the mental space you need to focus on the things that truly matter.

Simple living can save you money. When you're intentional with your spending and focus on buying only what you truly need and value, you can save a significant amount of money over time. This can free you up to pursue other goals and priorities, whether that's traveling, starting a business, or simply building up your savings.

Simple living can be better for the planet. When we consume less and focus on using what we have in a mindful and sustainable way, we can reduce our environmental impact and help create a more sustainable future.

Ultimately, simple living is about creating a life that is aligned with your values and brings you joy and fulfillment. It's not about depriving yourself or living in a state of constant self-denial. Rather, it's about consciously choosing to live with less in order to make room for more of what truly matters. In the pages that follow, we'll explore the many benefits of simple living and offer practical advice for incorporating this powerful philosophy into your own life.

The Benefits of Simple Living

Simplicity offers a wide range of benefits, both practical and psychological. The following are some of the key benefits of living a simple lifestyle:

Reduced stress and anxiety: Living in a cluttered and disorganized environment can be a source of stress and anxiety. Simplicity can help reduce stress by creating an orderly and calming space. When you have fewer possessions and a simplified environment, it can be easier to find what you need and maintain a sense of control over your space. Additionally, by reducing visual clutter, you can create a more peaceful and relaxing atmosphere.

More time and freedom: Simple living encourages intentional living and focusing on what is most important. By simplifying your life and eliminating distractions, you can free up more time and energy for the things that truly matter. This can include spending time with loved ones, pursuing your passions and hobbies, or investing in your personal and professional growth.

More financial stability: Simple living often involves being more mindful about your spending. By cutting out unnecessary purchases and focusing on what truly matters, you can save money and build more financial stability. This can lead to greater freedom and peace of mind when it comes to your finances.

Greater clarity and focus: A simple lifestyle helps you cut out distractions and focus on what's truly important. By reducing the clutter in your life, you can achieve greater clarity and focus on your goals. This can help you make more intentional decisions about how you spend your time and energy, and ensure that you are investing in the things that matter most to you.

Improved mental health: Simple living can help reduce feelings of overwhelm, anxiety, and depression. By simplifying your life, you can create a more peaceful and calming environment for your mental health. Additionally, by focusing on what truly matters and eliminating unnecessary stressors, you can reduce feelings of overwhelm and anxiety. This can lead to improved mood, increased happiness, and greater overall well-being.

Better physical health: Simple living encourages healthier habits, such as regular exercise, eating a healthy diet, and getting enough sleep. These healthy habits can improve your physical health and well-being. Additionally, by simplifying your environment, you can create a space that is conducive to physical health, such as an uncluttered home gym or a kitchen with only the essentials for healthy cooking.

More meaningful relationships: Simplicity emphasizes the importance of cultivating meaningful relationships and spending time with loved ones. By focusing on what truly matters, you can build deeper and more meaningful connections with others. This can include spending quality time with friends and family, volunteering in your community, or engaging in activities that align with your values and passions.

Positive impact on the environment: By consuming less and being more mindful about the things you buy and use, you can have a positive impact on the environment and reduce your carbon footprint. This can include buying fewer disposable products, reducing your energy consumption, and using public transportation or biking instead of driving.

Overall, Simple living can help you live a more intentional, fulfilling, and peaceful life, one that is grounded in your true priorities and values. By simplifying your environment and focusing on what truly matters, you can create a life that is aligned with your goals and values, and experience greater happiness and well-being as a result.

Understanding Clutter

Marie Kondo, a Japanese organizing consultant, and author of the best-selling book "The Life-Changing Magic of Tidying Up" was interested in organizing from a young age and began studying tidying methods as a teenager. She became a consultant in 2004 and established her own consulting business in Tokyo.

In her work with clients, Marie Kondo noticed that many people struggled with clutter and disorganization, which she believed was often a result of a lack of awareness about what truly brings joy and meaning into their lives. She developed the KonMari method, a unique approach to tidying that emphasizes keeping only those items that spark joy and discarding the rest.

Marie Kondo's book became an international best-seller and inspired millions of people to declutter their homes and lives. She encourages her clients to take a mindful approach to their belongings, thanking them for their service and letting them go with gratitude for the role they played in their lives.

In addition to her book, Marie Kondo has become a cultural phenomenon, appearing on talk shows and starring in her own Netflix series, "Tidying Up with Marie Kondo." Her story is a powerful reminder that clutter can be a physical manifestation of emotional baggage and that decluttering can lead to a more peaceful and intentional way of living.

Clutter refers to the accumulation of excess items in a space that serve no useful purpose or have no significant value. Clutter can be physical, such as piles of paper, clothes, or household items, or it can be digital, such as an overflowing inbox or numerous unused apps on a phone or computer.

Clutter can have negative effects on our physical and mental well-being. Physical clutter can create a sense of disorganization and chaos, making it difficult to find what you need and complete tasks efficiently. It can also be a safety hazard, as cluttered spaces can lead to falls and injuries.

Mental clutter can also be detrimental, as it can create feelings of overwhelm, stress, and anxiety. When we are surrounded by clutter, it can be difficult to focus on what's truly important and make intentional decisions about how to spend our time and energy. Additionally, clutter can be a source of guilt and shame, as it can remind us of unfinished tasks or unfulfilled obligations.

Understanding clutter is an important first step in living a minimalist lifestyle. By recognizing the negative impact that clutter can have on our lives, we can begin to take action to simplify our environment and create a more peaceful and intentional life. This may involve decluttering our physical and digital spaces, establishing habits to prevent future clutter, and focusing on what truly matters in our lives.

There are various types of clutter that can accumulate in our physical and digital spaces. Here are some common types of clutter:

Type of clutter

Emotional clutter: These are items that we hold onto for emotional reasons, such as old photographs, letters, or mementos. While these items may hold emotional value, they can also take up valuable space and contribute to clutter.

Paper clutter: This includes stacks of old bills, magazines, and mail that can accumulate over time. Paper clutter can create a sense of disorganization and make it difficult to find important documents when needed.

Clothing clutter: This type of clutter refers to clothes that are no longer worn or don't fit properly, yet are still kept in the closet. Clothing clutter can take up valuable space and make it difficult to find and wear the clothes that are truly important.

Digital clutter: This includes unused apps, old files, and unread emails that can accumulate on our phones and computers. Digital clutter can slow down devices and make it difficult to find important information when needed.

Hobby clutter: This type of clutter refers to items associated with hobbies or collections, such as sports equipment, crafting supplies, or memorabilia. While these items may bring joy, they can also take up valuable space and contribute to clutter.

Household clutter: This includes excess furniture, decor, and household items that may not serve a useful purpose or add value to your home.

Understanding the types of clutter that may be present in your life can help you identify areas where you can simplify and declutter. By focusing on the types of clutter that are most prevalent in your life, you can develop strategies to prevent future clutter and create a more intentional and peaceful environment.

The Impact of Clutter on Your Life

Tracy McCubbin, a decluttering expert and author of the book "Making Space, Clutter Free." Tracy grew up in a cluttered home and struggled with disorganization and clutter throughout her life. She became a professional organizer and founded her own company, dClutterfly, in Los Angeles.

Tracy's work with clients has shown that clutter can have a profound impact on our lives, affecting our physical and emotional health, our relationships, and our productivity. In her book, she shares stories of clients who have transformed their lives through decluttering, including one woman who was able to pursue her dream of starting a business after clearing out the clutter in her home office.

Tracy's own life has been transformed by decluttering as well. She shares in her book how she was able to heal from the trauma of her mother's death by decluttering her childhood home and letting go of the physical reminders of her past. She also experienced improved mental and physical health as a result of living in a clutter-free environment.

The impact of decluttering is not just anecdotal; studies have shown that clutter can lead to increased stress, decreased productivity, and even physical health problems. Decluttering can have a positive impact on our lives, improving our mental and physical health, increasing our productivity, and helping us to create a more peaceful and intentional way of living.

Tracy's story is a powerful example of the transformative power of decluttering and a reminder that letting go of physical clutter can lead to a more joyful and fulfilling life.

Clutter can have a significant impact on our physical, mental, and emotional well-being. Here are some ways that clutter can affect your life:

Stress and anxiety: Imagine coming home after a long day of work to a cluttered and disorganized living space. There are piles of mail and paperwork on the kitchen counter, clothes strewn about the bedroom, and toys and books scattered throughout the living room. This chaotic environment can create a sense of overwhelm and contribute to feelings of stress and anxiety.

Poor health: If you live in a cluttered and disorganized home, you may be more likely to experience health problems. For example, if you have stacks of clutter on the floor, it can be difficult to navigate your living space safely and you may be more prone to tripping and falling. Clutter can also make it difficult to clean and maintain a healthy living space, leading to issues like allergies and respiratory problems.

Decreased productivity: If you work from home and your workspace is cluttered, it can be difficult to focus and complete tasks efficiently. For example, if you have papers and files stacked up on your desk, it can be difficult to find what you need and complete work on time. This can have negative impacts on your work and your ability to achieve your goals.

Guilt and shame: If you have a cluttered closet full of clothes that you no longer wear, it can be a source of guilt and shame. Every time you open the closet door, you may be reminded of the money you spent on those items and the wasted space they are taking up in your home.

Financial burden: If you have a cluttered home, you may be more likely to spend money on unnecessary items or storage solutions. For example, if you have a cluttered closet, you may be tempted to purchase more storage containers or shelves to help organize your belongings. This can create a financial burden and contribute to feelings of stress and overwhelm.

You can begin to take action to declutter and simplify your environment by understanding how clutter can impact different areas of your life. You can improve your physical and mental well-being, increase your productivity, and reduce stress and anxiety in your life by eliminating clutter.

Decluttering Your Home

Decluttering your home is an essential step in simplifying your life and living a minimalist lifestyle. In this chapter, we'll explore some practical tips and strategies for decluttering your home and creating a more intentional and peaceful living space.

Set a goal: Before you begin decluttering, it's important to set a clear goal for yourself. Determine what areas of your home you want to declutter and how much time and effort you want to invest in the process. Setting a goal can help you stay focused and motivated throughout the decluttering process.

Start small: Decluttering your entire home can feel overwhelming, so it's important to start small and work your way up. Begin with one room or one area of your home, such as a closet or a bookshelf. Once you've successfully decluttered that space, move on to the next.

Sort items into categories: As you declutter, sort your items into categories such as "keep," "donate," and "discard." This can help you make more efficient and effective decisions about what to keep and what to let go of.

Consider the 80/20 rule: The 80/20 rule, also known as the Pareto principle, suggests that we use 20% of our possessions 80% of the time. Consider this rule as you declutter and ask yourself if you really need or use the items that are taking up space in your home.

Let go of sentimental items: Sentimental items such as old letters or childhood toys can be difficult to let go of, but they can also take up valuable space in your home. Consider taking a photo of the item as a way to preserve the memory and then donate or discard the physical item.

Create a designated donation area: As you sort through your items, create a designated area in your home for items you plan to donate. This can make it easier to drop off donations at a later time and can also help you see the progress you're making.

Consider your future needs: When decluttering, it's important to consider your future needs and lifestyle. For example, if you plan to move to a smaller home or travel frequently, you may need to let go of more items than someone who plans to stay in a larger home long-term.

Decluttering your home can be a challenging process, but it can also be incredibly rewarding. By letting go of excess possessions and creating a more intentional living space, you can reduce stress and anxiety in your life and create more time and energy for the things that matter most.

The KonMari Method

The KonMari Method, developed by Japanese organizing consultant Marie Kondo, has become a popular approach to decluttering and simplifying homes around the world. Here, we'll explore the key principles of the KonMari Method and how you can apply them to your own decluttering process.

Start with clothing: According to the KonMari Method, the first step in decluttering your home is to start with your clothing. Gather all of your clothing items in one place and go through each item, asking yourself if it brings you joy. If it doesn't, it's time to let it go.

Focus on joy: The KonMari Method is centered around the idea of keeping only items that bring you joy. When going through your possessions, hold each item in your hands and ask yourself if it sparks joy. If it does, keep it. If it doesn't, thank it for its service and let it go.

Tidy by category, not location: Rather than tackling one room or area at a time, the KonMari Method encourages tidying by category. This means going through all of your books, for example, rather than just the ones in your living room. By tidying by category, you can see all of your possessions in one place and make more intentional decisions about what to keep and what to let go of.

Follow a specific order: The KonMari Method follows a specific order for decluttering: clothing, books, papers, komono (miscellaneous items), and sentimental items. By following this order, you can build momentum and make the decluttering process easier over time.

Use storage solutions wisely: The KonMari Method emphasizes the importance of storing items in a way that allows you to see and access them easily. Use storage solutions such as boxes or bins to keep items organized, and fold clothes in a way that allows you to see each item clearly.

Focus on the present and future: When decluttering, it's important to focus on your present and future needs rather than dwelling on the past. Letting go of items that no longer bring you joy can create space for new experiences and opportunities in your life.

The KonMari Method has helped countless people simplify their homes and live more intentionally. By focusing on joy and following a specific order for decluttering, you can create a more peaceful and intentional living space.

Tips for letting go emotional items

Letting go of emotional items can be one of the most difficult parts of decluttering, but it's an important step towards living a more minimalist lifestyle. Here are some tips to help you let go of emotional items:

Take your time: It's okay to take your time when going through emotional items. Allow yourself to feel the emotions that come up, and take breaks when needed.

Choose carefully: When deciding which emotional items to keep, choose carefully. Keep only the items that truly hold meaning for you and bring you joy.

Take photos: Consider taking photos of emotional items that you don't want to keep. This way, you can still hold onto the memories without holding onto the physical item.

Repurpose or donate: Consider repurposing emotional items into something new or donating them to someone who can use them. This can help you feel like the item is still being put to good use.

Create a memory box: If you're struggling to let go of emotional items, consider creating a memory box to store them in. Choose a small box or container and limit yourself to keeping only the most meaningful items.

Write down memories: Sometimes just writing down memories can be enough to help you let go of emotional items. Consider journaling about the item or writing a letter to yourself or someone else about the memories associated with it.

Although letting go of emotional items can be difficult, but it can also be freeing. By keeping only the items that truly bring you joy and letting go of the rest, you can create space for new experiences and memories in your life.

Donating, Selling, or Recycling Your Clutter

When decluttering your home, you may find that you have a lot of items that you no longer need or want. Instead of throwing them away, consider donating, selling, or recycling them. Here are some tips for each option:

Donating: Donating your items is a great way to give back to your community and help those in need. Look for local charities or non-profit organizations that accept donations, such as Goodwill or the Salvation Army. You can also donate items to homeless shelters, women's shelters, or animal shelters. Be sure to check with each organization to see what items they accept and how to donate them.

Selling: If you have items that are still in good condition, consider selling them. You can hold a garage sale, sell items online through platforms like Facebook Marketplace, Craigslist, or eBay, or take them to a consignment shop. Be sure to price your items fairly and be prepared to negotiate with buyers.

Recycling: Recycling is a great way to reduce waste and give new life to old items. Check with your local recycling center or waste management facility to see what items they accept for recycling. Some items that can be recycled include paper, cardboard, plastic, metal, and electronics.

When deciding what to do with your clutter, it's important to choose the option that is best for you and your items. Donating, selling, or recycling your clutter can not only help you clear out your space, but it can also benefit others and the environment.

Simplifying Your Schedule

Simplifying your schedule can have many benefits, including reducing stress and creating more time for the things that matter most to you. Here are some reasons why you simplify should simplify your schedule:

Reduce stress: A busy schedule can lead to stress and burnout. By simplifying your schedule, you can reduce the number of commitments and responsibilities you have, which can lead to less stress and more peace of mind.

Create more time: Simplifying your schedule can also create more time for the things that are most important to you, such as spending time with family and friends, pursuing hobbies and interests, or simply relaxing and taking care of yourself.

Improve focus: A simpler schedule can help you focus on the tasks and activities that are most important to you, rather than feeling overwhelmed and scattered by a long to-do list.

Here are some tips for simplifying your schedule:

Prioritize: Make a list of the things that are most important to you and prioritize them. This will help you focus on what truly matters and eliminate activities that are less important.

Learn to say no: Saying no can be difficult, but it's an important skill to learn when simplifying your schedule. Be honest with yourself about what you can realistically take on and don't be afraid to say no to things that don't align with your priorities.

Delegate: If you have too many responsibilities, consider delegating some of them to others. This could mean hiring a house cleaner, asking a friend or family member for help with a task, or delegating work tasks to a colleague.

Create boundaries: Set boundaries around your time and commitments. For example, limit the number of social events you attend each week, or set aside specific times for work and personal tasks.

By simplifying your schedule, you can reduce stress, create more time for the things that matter, and improve your focus and productivity. It may take some time and effort to make these changes, but the benefits are well worth it.

The Importance of Prioritization

Prioritization is a critical skill for personal and professional success. It involves identifying what is most important and focusing your time and resources on those tasks or activities. Here are some reasons why prioritization is so important:

Increases productivity: By prioritizing your tasks, you can focus on the most important and high-impact activities, which can lead to increased productivity and efficiency.

Helps achieve goals: Prioritization helps you to align your tasks and activities with your goals and objectives. By focusing on the tasks that are most critical to achieving your goals, you are more likely to be successful.

Reduces stress: When you have a long to-do list with many competing priorities, it can be overwhelming and stressful. Prioritizing your tasks can help you to identify what needs to be done first, which can reduce stress and increase your sense of control over your workload.

Enables effective time management: Time is a finite resource, and prioritization helps you to make the most of your time. By focusing on the most important tasks, you can allocate your time effectively and ensure that you are spending your time on activities that align with your goals.

Improves decision-making: Prioritization requires you to make decisions about what is most important and what can wait. This helps you to develop your decision-making skills and become more confident in your ability to make important choices.

In summary, prioritization is a critical skill for success in all areas of life. It helps to increase productivity, achieve goals, reduce stress, enable effective time management, and improve decision-making. By learning to prioritize effectively, you can make the most of your time and resources and achieve your goals more efficiently.

Strategies for Saying No

Saying "no" can be difficult, but it is an important skill to develop. Here are some strategies for saying no:

Be clear and direct: When saying no, be clear and direct. Don't beat around the bush or give false hope. Say what you mean and mean what you say.

Explain why: When turning down a request or invitation, it can be helpful to explain why you are saying no. Be honest and clear about your reasons.

Offer an alternative: If you can't say yes to a request, consider offering an alternative solution. For example, if you can't attend a meeting, offer to participate via phone or video conference.

Prioritize: When deciding whether to say yes or no to a request, consider your priorities. Is this request in line with your goals and values? If not, it may be easier to say no.

Practice: Saying no can be uncomfortable, especially if you are used to saying yes to everything. Practice saying no in low-stakes situations so that you can build your confidence and become more comfortable with the process.

Be respectful: When saying no, be respectful and kind. Show empathy for the person making the request and thank them for thinking of you.

Saying no is not a personal rejection. It is simply a decision to prioritize your time and resources. By developing the skill of saying no, you can reduce stress, increase productivity, and maintain healthy boundaries.

Managing Your Time Effectively

Managing your time effectively is a key skill for success in all areas of life. Here are some strategies for managing your time effectively:

Prioritize: As discussed earlier, prioritizing your tasks is critical for effective time management.

Identify the most important tasks and focus your time and energy on those.

Set goals: Setting goals helps you to focus your time and efforts on what is most important. Set both short-term and long-term goals, and break them down into smaller, manageable tasks.

Create a schedule: Create a schedule or to-do list to help you stay organized and on track. Make sure to schedule in breaks and downtime to help you recharge.

Use a planner: A planner can help you to keep track of your schedule, appointments, and deadlines. Use it to plan out your day, week, and month.

Avoid distractions: Distractions can be a major time-waster. Minimize distractions by turning off notifications on your phone and computer, closing your office door, or finding a quiet space to work.

Learn to delegate: Delegating tasks to others can help you to free up time and focus on what is most important. Identify tasks that can be delegated to others and find trusted individuals to take them on.

Take breaks: Taking breaks can actually help you to be more productive. Make sure to take regular breaks throughout the day to recharge and refocus.

Time is a finite resource, and managing it effectively is critical for success. By prioritizing, setting goals, creating a schedule, avoiding distractions, delegating, and taking breaks, you can make the most of your time and achieve your goals more efficiently.

Streamlining Your Finances

Streamlining your finances is an important part of achieving financial stability and freedom. Here are some strategies for streamlining your finances:

Create a budget: A budget is a critical tool for managing your finances. It helps you to track your income and expenses, identify areas where you can cut costs, and set goals for saving and investing.

Automate your finances: Automating your finances can help you to save time and avoid missed payments. Set up automatic bill payments, savings transfers, and investment contributions.

Consolidate your accounts: If you have multiple bank accounts, credit cards, or investment accounts, consider consolidating them to simplify your finances. This can help you to keep track of your money more easily and avoid confusion.

Reduce debt: Reducing debt is a key part of streamlining your finances. Make a plan to pay off high-interest debt first, and consider consolidating or refinancing loans to reduce interest rates.

Cut unnecessary expenses: Identify areas where you can cut expenses, such as dining out, entertainment, or subscriptions. Consider negotiating bills, switching to a cheaper service provider, or finding free alternatives.

Increase your income: Increasing your income can help you to achieve your financial goals more quickly. Consider asking for a raise, starting a side hustle, or investing in education or training to increase your earning potential.

Streamlining your finances takes time and effort, but it can help you to achieve financial stability and freedom. By creating a budget, automating your finances, consolidating accounts, reducing debt, cutting unnecessary expenses, and increasing your income, you can take control of your finances and achieve your financial goals.

Budgeting basics

Budgeting is a key part of managing your finances effectively. Here are some budgeting basics to help you get started:

Track your income: The first step in creating a budget is to track your income. This includes all sources of income, such as your salary, investments, and any side hustles or freelance work.

List your expenses: Next, make a list of all your monthly expenses. This includes fixed expenses like rent, utilities, and loan payments, as well as variable expenses like groceries, dining out, and entertainment.

Categorize your expenses: Once you have listed all your expenses, categorize them into essential and non-essential expenses. Essential expenses are those that you need to pay to live, while non-essential expenses are those that are nice to have but not necessary.

Set a budget: Based on your income and expenses, set a budget for each category. Be realistic and make sure to leave some room for unexpected expenses.

Track your spending: Once you have set your budget, track your spending to see how well you are sticking to it. This can help you to identify areas where you need to cut back or make adjustments.

Review and adjust: Review your budget regularly, and make adjustments as needed. If you are consistently overspending in a particular category, you may need to cut back or find ways to increase your income.

Budgeting is a tool to help you manage your finances and achieve your financial goals. By tracking your income and expenses, categorizing your expenses, setting a budget, tracking your spending, and reviewing and adjusting your budget regularly, you can take control of your finances and achieve financial stability and freedom.

Reducing Debt

Reducing debt is an important part of achieving financial stability and freedom. Here are some strategies for reducing debt:

Prioritize high-interest debt: If you have multiple debts, prioritize paying off the ones with the highest interest rates first. This will help you to save money on interest and pay off your debt faster.

Create a debt repayment plan: Develop a plan for how you will pay off your debt. This may involve increasing your income, reducing your expenses, or a combination of both. Consider using the debt snowball or debt avalanche method to pay off your debt systematically.

Cut back on expenses: Look for ways to cut back on your expenses and redirect the money towards paying off your debt. This may involve reducing your discretionary spending, negotiating bills, or finding ways to lower your fixed expenses.

Increase your income: Consider taking on a side hustle, freelancing, or finding ways to increase your income. Any extra money you earn can be put towards paying off your debt faster.

Consolidate or refinance debt: If you have multiple debts, consolidating or refinancing them may help you to save money on interest and reduce your monthly payments. Be sure to research the options available and choose the one that makes the most financial sense for you.

Seek professional help: If you are struggling with debt, consider seeking professional help from a credit counseling agency or a financial advisor. They can provide guidance and support in developing a debt repayment plan and managing your finances.

Reducing debt takes time and effort, but it is an important step towards achieving financial stability and freedom. By prioritizing high-interest debt, creating a debt repayment plan, cutting back on expenses, increasing your income, consolidating or refinancing debt, and seeking professional help when needed, you can take control of your finances and reduce your debt over time.

Living Within Your Means

Living within your means is a fundamental principle of personal finance that involves spending less money than you earn. By living within your means, you can avoid debt, build savings, and achieve financial stability. Here are some strategies for living within your means:

Create a budget: Start by creating a budget that tracks your income and expenses. This will help you to identify areas where you can cut back on expenses and redirect your money towards savings or debt repayment.

Prioritize needs over wants: When making purchase decisions, prioritize your needs over your wants. This means focusing on the things that are essential for your survival and well-being, such as housing, food, and healthcare.

Reduce unnecessary expenses: Look for ways to reduce unnecessary expenses, such as cutting back on dining out, entertainment, or subscription services. Small changes can add up over time and make a big difference in your finances.

Avoid debt: Avoid taking on debt whenever possible. If you need to borrow money, choose the option with the lowest interest rate and pay it off as quickly as possible.

Build an emergency fund: Start building an emergency fund that can cover unexpected expenses such as medical bills, car repairs, or job loss. Aim to save three to six months' worth of living expenses in your emergency fund.

Increase your income: Look for ways to increase your income, such as taking on a side job or starting a small business. This can help you to build savings and achieve your financial goals more quickly.

Living within your means requires discipline and a willingness to make sacrifices. By creating a budget, prioritizing needs over wants, reducing unnecessary expenses, avoiding debt, building an emergency fund, and increasing your income, you can take control of your finances and live a more financially stable life.

Cultivating Minimalist Habits

Cultivating minimalist habits is an essential step towards living a simple lifestyle. Here are some strategies for developing minimalist habits:

Start small: Begin by decluttering one area of your home or one aspect of your life, such as your wardrobe or your digital devices. This will help you to build momentum and develop the habit of simplifying your life.

Develop a routine: Establish a daily or weekly routine for decluttering and organizing your home and your life. This will help you to stay on track and make progress towards your minimalist goals.

Adopt simplicity in all areas of your life: Simplicity is not just about decluttering your physical space, but also about simplifying your schedule, your finances, and your relationships. Look for ways to incorporate minimalist principles into all areas of your life.

Focus on experiences over possessions: Instead of accumulating material possessions, focus on experiences that bring you joy and fulfillment. This could be traveling, spending time with loved ones, or pursuing a hobby or passion.

Practice mindfulness: Mindfulness can help you to become more aware of your thoughts and actions, and make intentional choices that align with your values and goals. Incorporate mindfulness practices such as meditation or journaling into your daily routine.

Be intentional with your purchases: Before making a purchase, ask yourself if it aligns with your values and if it will truly bring value to your life. Avoid impulse purchases and focus on buying high-quality items that will last.

Simple living is a journey, not a destination. It takes time, practice, and dedication to develop these habits and make them a part of your everyday life. By starting small, developing a routine, embracing simplicity in all areas of your life, focusing on experiences over possessions, practicing mindfulness, and being intentional with your purchases, you can create a more intentional and fulfilling life.

Mindful Consumption

Mindful consumption is an essential part of living a simplistic lifestyle. It means being intentional and mindful of what you consume, whether it's food, products, or media.

Here are some strategies for practicing mindful consumption:

Slow down: Take time to consider your purchases and consumption habits. Avoid impulse buying and instead make intentional choices that align with your values and needs.

Practice gratitude: Appreciate what you have instead of constantly seeking more. Gratitude can help you develop a sense of contentment and reduce the urge to consume.

Buy less, but better: Focus on quality over quantity. Invest in high-quality, long-lasting items that will bring value to your life, rather than constantly buying cheap, disposable products.

Support ethical and sustainable brands: Choose brands that align with your values and prioritize ethical and sustainable practices. Consider factors such as the environmental impact of production, fair labor practices, and cruelty-free products.

Limit screen time: Be mindful of the media you consume, including social media, news, and entertainment. Set limits on your screen time and prioritize activities that nourish your mind and body.

Practice minimalism in your diet: Focus on whole, nutritious foods and avoid overconsumption of processed and packaged foods. This can help you develop a healthier and more sustainable relationship with food.

By practicing mindful consumption, you can reduce waste, save money, and develop a more intentional and fulfilling life.

Gratitude Practice

Gratitude practice is an essential part of living a simple lifestyle. It involves cultivating a sense of gratitude and appreciation for the people, experiences, and possessions in your life.

Here are some strategies for practicing gratitude:

Keep a gratitude journal: Write down three to five things you're grateful for each day. This can help you focus on the positive aspects of your life and develop a sense of appreciation.

Practice mindfulness: Take time each day to be present and mindful of your surroundings. Notice the beauty in everyday moments and appreciate the small things in life.

Express gratitude to others: Take time to thank the people in your life who have made a positive impact. Express your gratitude through a thank-you note, a kind word, or a small gift.

Practice self-care: Take care of yourself by engaging in activities that nourish your mind and body. This can include exercise, meditation, reading, or spending time in nature.

Develop a simplicity mindset: Focus on the things you have, rather than the things you don't have. Appreciate the simplicity of a minimalist lifestyle and the freedom it can bring.

By practicing gratitude, you can develop a more positive and fulfilling life. It can help you shift your focus away from material possessions and instead appreciate the people and experiences that truly matter.

Embracing Imperfection

Embracing imperfection is an essential part of living a minimalist lifestyle. It involves accepting yourself and others as they are, rather than striving for perfection. When you let go of the need to be perfect, you free yourself from the pressure of trying to do everything perfectly and can focus on what really matters.

Here are some strategies for embracing imperfection:

Recognize that perfection is impossible: No one is perfect, and striving for perfection is a recipe for disappointment and frustration. Accept that mistakes and imperfections are a natural part of life.

Practice self-compassion: Be kind to yourself when things don't go as planned. Treat yourself with the same kindness and understanding you would offer to a close friend.

Let go of expectations: Release your expectations of yourself and others. Recognize that everyone has their own strengths and weaknesses, and it's okay to not have everything figured out.

Focus on progress, not perfection: Instead of striving for perfection, focus on making progress towards your goals. Celebrate small victories and milestones along the way.

Adopt the beauty of imperfection: Imperfections can add character and charm to people and things. Learn to appreciate the unique qualities and imperfections that make you and others special.

By embracing imperfection, you can free yourself from the pressure of trying to be perfect and live a more authentic and fulfilling life. It can help you develop a sense of self-acceptance and compassion towards others, creating deeper connections and relationships.

Living a Minimalist Lifestyle in the Real World

Living a simple life can be a challenge in the real world, where we are bombarded with advertisements and societal pressures to consume more. However, it is possible to maintain a minimalist lifestyle and still navigate the demands of everyday life.

Here are some tips for living a simple lifestyle in the real world:

Set boundaries: Be intentional about what you allow into your life. Learn to say "no" to things that don't align with your values or add value to your life.

Practice mindful consumption: Before making a purchase, ask yourself if it is something you truly need or will bring you joy. Consider the environmental and social impact of your purchases.

Develop gratitude: Focus on what you already have rather than what you lack. Gratitude can help you appreciate the things that truly matter in your life and reduce the urge to accumulate more.

Surround yourself with like-minded people: Connect with others who share your values and support your simple lifestyle. Join a similar lifestyle group or attend a minimalist event to meet others who are on a similar journey.

Simplify your routines: Identify areas of your life where you can simplify and streamline your routines. This can include meal planning, wardrobe selection, or household chores.

Practice self-care: Take care of yourself physically, emotionally, and mentally. Prioritize activities that bring you joy and fulfillment, and let go of those that drain your energy.

Living a Simple lifestyle in the real world requires intentionality and commitment, but it can lead to a more fulfilling and meaningful life. By prioritizing the things that truly matter and letting go of excess, you can create more space for the things that bring you joy and purpose.

Dealing with Pressure from Others

Simple living can sometimes lead to pressure from others who may not understand or agree with your choices. It is important to remember that ultimately, you are the one who is responsible for your own happiness and well-being.

Here are some tips for dealing with pressure from others:

Communicate your values: Explain to others why you have chosen to live a minimalist lifestyle and how it aligns with your values. Be open and honest about your reasons for making these choices.

Set boundaries: Be clear about your boundaries and what you are and are not willing to compromise on. You have the right to say "no" to things that do not align with your values or priorities.

Focus on your own journey: Everyone's journey is different, and it is not your job to convince others to live a simplicity lifestyle. Focus on your own choices and let others make their own decisions.

Seek support: Connect with others who share your values and can support you on your journey. Join a minimalist group or attend a minimalist event to meet others who are on a similar path.

Practice self-care: Take care of yourself physically, emotionally, and mentally. Prioritize activities that bring you joy and fulfillment, and let go of those that drain your energy.

Dealing with pressure from others can be challenging, but it is important to stay true to your values and priorities. By communicating your values, setting boundaries, and focusing on your own journey, you can live a minimalist lifestyle that is true to who you are.

Building a Support Network

Building a support network is essential for anyone who wants to successfully live a minimalist lifestyle. Having people in your life who understand and support your choices can make all the difference in staying committed to your goals.

Here are some tips for building a support network:

Find like-minded individuals: Seek out people who share your values and are also interested in living a simple lifestyle. Joining a local minimalist group or attending a minimalist event can be a great way to meet others who share your interests.

Connect with family and friends: Explain to your loved ones why you are pursuing a simple lifestyle and how it will benefit you. Ask for their support and encouragement.

Use social media: Social media can be a powerful tool for connecting with others who share your interests. Follow minimalist influencers and bloggers, and join minimalist groups on social media.

Attend workshops or classes: Consider attending a workshop or class on minimalism. This can be a great way to meet like-minded individuals and learn more about living a minimalist lifestyle.

Find a mentor: Seek out someone who has successfully transitioned to a minimalist lifestyle and ask them to be your mentor. They can provide valuable guidance and support as you navigate this new way of living.

Building a support network takes time and effort, but it is worth it in the end. By surrounding yourself with people who understand and support your choices, you can stay motivated and committed to living a minimalist lifestyle.

Creating Your Own Definition of Simple Living

While there are common themes and principles associated with simple lifestyles, it's important to create your own definition of simple living. The concept of simple living means different things to different people, and there's no one-size-fits-all approach to living a simple lifestyle.

Here are some tips for creating your own definition of simple living:

Reflect on your values: Consider what's important to you and what you want to prioritize in your life. Simple living is about living intentionally and aligning your actions with your values.

Identify your goals: Think about what you hope to achieve by pursuing a simple lifestyle. Are you looking to simplify your life, reduce stress, or live more sustainably? By setting goals, you can create a clear vision for what simple living means to you.

Define your own rules: Decide what you want to keep and what you want to let go of in your life. This can include physical possessions, time commitments, and even relationships. Creating your own rules will help you stay true to your values and goals.

Be flexible: Your definition of simple living may change over time. Be open to new experiences and ideas, and don't be afraid to adjust your approach as needed.

Accept imperfection: Simple living is not about achieving perfection. It's about living intentionally and with purpose. Accept that there will be setbacks and challenges along the way, and that's okay.

By creating your own definition of simple living, you can customize the concept to fit your unique needs and circumstances. This will help you stay motivated and committed to living a simple lifestyle that's truly meaningful to you.

Successful Minimalistic

- Marie Kondo is a Japanese organizing consultant and author who has helped millions of people declutter their homes and lives through her "KonMari" method. Her approach is focused on identifying and keeping only the things that "spark joy" in our lives, and letting go of the rest. By simplifying our physical spaces and surrounding ourselves only with things that bring us happiness, Kondo believes we can create a more peaceful and joyful life.

- Leo Babauta is the author of the popular blog "Zen Habits," which focuses on minimalism, simplicity, and mindfulness. His message is centered on the idea that by simplifying our lives and letting go of distractions, we can achieve greater focus, productivity, and happiness. Babauta's approach is practical and actionable, offering readers concrete steps they can take to simplify their lives and find greater fulfillment.

- Courtney and Hans Wilhelm are a couple who have adopted minimalism and simplified their lives by downsizing their home and possessions. Their journey started when they realized they were living a life that wasn't aligned with their values, and they decided to make a change. By decluttering their home and living with less, they have found greater happiness and fulfillment in their lives.

- Francine Jay, also known as "Miss Minimalist," is an author and blogger who has helped people around the world simplify their homes and lives. Her approach is focused on identifying what truly matters to us, and letting go of the rest. Jay believes that by decluttering our physical spaces and simplifying our lives, we can free up time, energy, and resources to focus on what really matters to us.

- Graham Hill is an entrepreneur and founder of the sustainable design company LifeEdited. Hill has designed small, minimalist living spaces that maximize functionality and sustainability. His approach is focused on creating spaces that are efficient, beautiful, and easy to maintain, while minimizing our impact on the environment.

- Courtney Carver is the author and founder of the minimalist fashion blog "Be More with Less." She has inspired people around the world to simplify their wardrobes and adopt a more intentional lifestyle. Carver believes that by owning fewer clothes and focusing on quality over quantity, we can simplify our lives, save money, and reduce our impact on the environment.

- Jess Lively is a blogger and podcaster who has adopted a minimalist lifestyle as a means of creating more joy, purpose, and fulfillment in her life. Her message is centered around the idea of living with intention and cultivating a deep connection to ourselves and others. Lively believes that by simplifying our lives and focusing on what truly matters, we can create a life that is truly meaningful and fulfilling.

- Josh Becker is a writer and speaker who has adopted minimalism as a means of simplifying his life and focusing on what truly matters. After experiencing a life-changing event that made him reevaluate his priorities, Becker decided to adopt minimalism and start living with less. He has since become a leading voice in the minimalist movement, and has authored several books on the topic, including "The More of Less" and "Simplify."

- Tammy Strobel is a writer and blogger who has adopted a minimalist lifestyle as a means of creating more freedom, joy, and fulfillment in her life. After experiencing a life-changing event, Strobel decided to downsize her possessions and adopt a simpler way of living. She has since authored several books on minimalism, including "You Can Buy Happiness (and It's Cheap)" and "Smalltopia," and has become a leading voice in the minimalist movement.

- Colin Wright is a writer, speaker, and entrepreneur who has adopted minimalism as a means of living a more intentional and fulfilling life. Wright is the author of several books on minimalism, including "Minimalism: Live a Meaningful Life" and "Some Thoughts About Relationships." His message is focused on the idea of letting go of the excess in our lives, and embracing a simpler way of living that is aligned with our values and priorities.

- President José Mujica of Uruguay: Mujica was known for his minimalist lifestyle during his presidency, choosing to live in a modest farmhouse rather than the presidential palace. He also donated a significant portion of his salary to charity and adopted sustainable living practices.

- Senator Elizabeth Warren of the United States: Warren has been vocal about her commitment to minimalism, including wearing the same outfit to campaign events and focusing on living a simple and frugal lifestyle.

- Mayor Eric Garcetti of Los Angeles: Garcetti has been known to live in a small apartment and ride his bike to work, embracing a minimalist lifestyle as a means of reducing his carbon footprint and living more sustainably.

- Steve Smith, former Australian cricket team captain: Smith has spoken publicly about his minimalist lifestyle, including how he lives out of a single suitcase during the cricket season and donates most of his clothes to charity.

- Jesse Itzler, former professional basketball player: Itzler is an entrepreneur and author who has written about his experiences living with a monk for 15 days and how it helped him Accept a more minimalist and intentional lifestyle.

Conclusion

Simple living is not just about reducing physical possessions or simplifying schedules. It's about living intentionally, with purpose and clarity, and focusing on what truly matters to us. When we adopt a minimalist mindset, we can reduce stress, improve our mental and emotional well-being, and create more time and space for the things that bring us joy and fulfillment.

By decluttering our homes and letting go of unnecessary possessions, we can create a more peaceful and organized living environment that promotes relaxation and creativity. Simplifying our schedules can help us avoid burnout and overwhelm, and allow us to focus on the things that truly matter, such as spending time with loved ones, pursuing our passions, and taking care of ourselves.

Streamlining our finances by creating a budget, reducing debt, and living within our means can free us from the stress and anxiety of financial burden, and allow us to focus on our personal and professional goals.

Cultivating simple living habits, such as practicing mindful consumption, expressing gratitude, and embracing imperfection, can help us stay grounded and focused on our values, even in the face of societal pressure and expectations.

By creating our own definition of simple living and building a support network of like-minded individuals, we can stay motivated and committed to simple living that's truly meaningful to us. In conclusion, living a simple lifestyle is about embracing simplicity, intentionality, and mindfulness, and creating a life that's full of purpose, joy, and fulfillment.

Self-Assessment

This self-assessment exercise is designed to help you gauge the extent to which simplicity is integrated into your life. Simple living is about finding joy in the essentials, decluttering both physically and mentally, and embracing a life of purpose and fulfillment. As you answer the following questions, consider your actions, habits, and mindset in relation to the principles of simplicity.

Guidelines:

Answer each question based on your current lifestyle and mindset.

Rate your responses on a scale of 1 to 5, where:

- *5 indicates a strong alignment with the principles of simple living.*
- *1 indicates an area where you might consider simplifying.*

Now, let's do on the self-assessment:

1) I prioritize experiences over material possessions in my life.

   A: Strongly Agree

   B: Agree

   C: Neutral

   D: Disagree

   E: Strongly Disagree

2) I find joy in the simple pleasures of life, such as nature, music, or a good book.

   A: Strongly Agree

   B: Agree

   C: Neutral

   D: Disagree

   E: Strongly Disagree

3) I am content with what I have and don't constantly seek more.

   A: Strongly Agree

   B: Agree

   C: Neutral

   D: Disagree

E: Strongly Disagree

4) I prefer a minimalist approach, keeping my living space clutter-free.

   A: Strongly Agree

   B: Agree

   C: Neutral

   D: Disagree

   E: Strongly Disagree

5) I value and prioritize meaningful relationships over a large social circle.

   A: Strongly Agree

   B: Agree

   C: Neutral

   D: Disagree

   E: Strongly Disagree

6) I make time for mindfulness practices, such as meditation or quiet reflection.

   A: Strongly Agree

   B: Agree

   C: Neutral

   D: Disagree

   E: Strongly Disagree

7) I am conscious of my environmental impact and strive to live sustainably.

A: Strongly Agree

B: Agree

C: Neutral

D: Disagree

E: Strongly Disagree

8) I am comfortable saying "no" to commitments that don't align with my values.

A: Strongly Agree

B: Agree

C: Neutral

D: Disagree

E: Strongly Disagree

9) I find fulfillment in the present moment rather than constantly planning for the future.

A: Strongly Agree

B: Agree

C: Neutral

D: Disagree

E: Strongly Disagree

10) I practice gratitude regularly, appreciating the small joys in life.

A: Strongly Agree

B: Agree

C: Neutral

D: Disagree

E: Strongly Disagree

11) I prioritize quality over quantity in my possessions and relationships.

A: Strongly Agree

B: Agree

C: Neutral

D: Disagree

E: Strongly Disagree

12) I enjoy spending time in nature and find it rejuvenating.

A: Strongly Agree

B: Agree

C: Neutral

D: Disagree

E: Strongly Disagree

13) I practice financial mindfulness, avoiding unnecessary expenses.

A: Strongly Agree

B: Agree

C: Neutral

D: Disagree

E: Strongly Disagree

14) I am open to simplifying my daily routines for greater efficiency.

A: Strongly Agree

B: Agree

C: Neutral

D: Disagree

E: Strongly Disagree

15) I accept imperfection and understand that mistakes are part of life.

A: Strongly Agree

B: Agree

C: Neutral

D: Disagree

E: Strongly Disagree

16) I find joy in giving back to my community or contributing to a cause.

A: Strongly Agree

B: Agree

C: Neutral

D: Disagree

E: Strongly Disagree

17) I am mindful of my digital consumption, limiting screen time.

A: Strongly Agree

B: Agree

C: Neutral

D: Disagree

E: Strongly Disagree

18) I prioritize self-care and well-being, recognizing its importance.

A: Strongly Agree

B: Agree

C: Neutral

D: Disagree

E: Strongly Disagree

19) I am open to letting go of possessions that no longer serve a purpose.

A: Strongly Agree

B: Agree

C: Neutral

D: Disagree

E: Strongly Disagree

20) I make time for activities that bring me joy and relaxation regularly.

A: Strongly Agree

B: Agree

C: Neutral

D: Disagree

E: Strongly Disagree

21) I find fulfillment in moments of stillness and quiet reflection.

A: Strongly Agree

B: Agree

C: Neutral

D: Disagree

E: Strongly Disagree

22) I am comfortable saying 'no' to commitments that overwhelm me.

A: Strongly Agree

B: Agree

C: Neutral

D: Disagree

E: Strongly Disagree

23) I practice gratitude regularly, acknowledging the positive aspects of my life.

A: Strongly Agree

B: Agree

C: Neutral

D: Disagree

E: Strongly Disagree

24) I value experiences over material possessions.

A: Strongly Agree

B: Agree

C: Neutral

D: Disagree

E: Strongly Disagree

25) I develop meaningful connections with others, focusing on quality relationships.

A: Strongly Agree

B: Agree

C: Neutral

D: Disagree

E: Strongly Disagree

26) I am conscious of my environmental impact and strive to reduce my carbon footprint.

A: Strongly Agree

B: Agree

C: Neutral

D: Disagree

E: Strongly Disagree

27) I set clear boundaries to protect my time and energy.

A: Strongly Agree

B: Agree

C: Neutral

D: Disagree

E: Strongly Disagree

28) I appreciate the beauty in simplicity and minimalist aesthetics.

A: Strongly Agree

B: Agree

C: Neutral

D: Disagree

E: Strongly Disagree

29) I actively seek opportunities for personal growth and self-improvement.

A: Strongly Agree

B: Agree

C: Neutral

D: Disagree

E: Strongly Disagree

30) I am content with what I have and seldom compare myself to others.

A: Strongly Agree

B: Agree

C: Neutral

D: Disagree

E: Strongly Disagree

Finally, reflect on your responses and consider how you can integrate simplicity into your life, adopting a more intentional and fulfilling existence. The goal is not perfection but progress in creating a life aligned with your values. Enjoy the journey toward simplicity!

Join My Community

https://community.askpndas.com/

Made in the USA
Columbia, SC
18 June 2025